Viganò vs. the Vatican

✠ ✠ ✠

Marco Tosatti

Viganò vs. the Vatican

The Uncensored Testimony
of the Italian Journalist
Who Helped Break the Story

✠ ✠ ✠

Translated by
Giuseppe Pellegrino

An imprint of Sophia Institute Press
Manchester, New Hampshire

Sophia Institute Press
Box 5284, Manchester, NH 03108
1-800-888-9344

www.SophiaInstitute.com

Sophia Institute Press® is a registered trademark of Sophia Institute.

Library of Congress Cataloging-in-Publication Data
To come.

First printing

Contents

✠ ✠ ✠

Viganò vs. the Vatican

✠ ✠ ✠

The Origin of the Drama

✠ ✠ ✠

✠ ✠ ✠

The story of the Viganò dossier, and of everything that followed, began for me one morning at the end of July 2018. A friend phoned me, asking me if I had read an article about the McCarrick[1] affair on a website that follows the Vatican and has close ties to the Secretariat of State.

Cardinal Theodore McCarrick, an American cardinal, had been accused in a civil case of abuse of a minor many years ago and, as a result, had been disciplined by the Vatican, which stripped him of his red hat and ordered him to live a life of seclusion, prayer, and penance—all this after many years of traveling the world and acting as an unofficial ambassador of the Holy See.

---

[1] Theodore Edward McCarrick (b. 1930) was archbishop of Washington from 2001 to 2006, when he retired. In June 2018, he was removed from public ministry because of credible sexual misconduct allegations. In July 2018, he resigned from the College of Cardinals, and in February 2019, he was laicized.

I had not read the article, so my friend summed it up for me.

Further, he said, Archbishop Viganò[2] would call me. He was angry about the references that were made in the article to the two nuncios to the United States who preceded him, who were both dead and could no longer speak for themselves, as well as references to Pope Benedict XVI, who had punished McCarrick.

I had met Carlo Maria Viganò a few times at social events and made his acquaintance, nothing more. My friend told me that Archbishop Viganò followed my blog *Stilum Curiae*,[3] and it seemed to him that, because I had the liberty to speak freely about Church matters, I might be the right person to do an interview with him.

I responded, "Why not?"

So a couple of days later, the archbishop called me. We agreed to meet at my house in Rome. He came one morning, and as I showed him my recorder, I told him that everything was ready for the interview.

---

[2] Now retired, Archbishop Carlo Maria Viganò (b. 1941) was secretary-general of the Governorate of Vatican City State from July 2009 to September 2011 and then apostolic nuncio to the United States from October 2011 to April 2016.

[3] https://www.marcotosatti.com/.

"No," he replied, "not yet. First I want to tell you a story."

We sat down, and he told me everything that you will soon read here in his first testimony. At the end, I asked, "So, shall we do the interview?"

Still he replied, "No. First I need to take care of some personal matters in the next few days."

✠ ✠ ✠

We met again a few days later.

A bit more time passed, and then the report of the grand jury of Pennsylvania came out;[4] it spoke extensively about Cardinal Wuerl,[5] one of the reigning pontiff's factotums in the United States, and so I took the initiative of calling Monsignor Viganò.

"Have you seen that the report of the grand jury came out?" I asked. "If you still intend to do that interview, perhaps this is the right moment."

---

[4] The August 14, 2018, report of the grand jury of Pennsylvania showed that in the previous seventy years, more than three hundred priests in six dioceses in Pennsylvania were accused of having sexually abused children.

[5] Cardinal Donald William Wuerl (b. 1940) was archbishop of Washington, D.C., from 2006 to 2018, when he resigned from that position.

7

He responded: "See you next week."

He arrived at my house once again and immediately said, "I thought I should write something instead of giving an interview. Would you like to read it?" We read the text through together twice, doing essential editing to clarify terms and concepts for nonspecialists and to remove superfluous lines.

We then considered which Italian newspaper should publish it. I thought of *La Verità*, as I held Maurizio Belpietro[6] in great esteem, and it seemed to me that it would be one of the few newspapers that would not sound the alarm to the Vatican to prevent its being published.

Viganò agreed; I called Belpietro, whom I did not know, and I explained to him the situation. He said he would be happy to publish the testimony. The archbishop also wanted it to be issued in English and Spanish. He knew Edward Pentin[7] and had spoken with him, and for Spanish publication I contacted Gabriel Ariza of Infovaticana. It would take a few days for the translations, as there were more than ten pages of text.

---

[6] Maurizio Belpietro (b. 1958): editor of the Italian newspaper *La Verità*.

[7] Edward Pentin has spent over a decade as the Rome correspondent for Catholic newspapers, including an American paper, the *National Catholic Register*.

Monsignor Viganò and I met on August 22 and decided that the testimony should be issued four days later, at 7:00 on Sunday morning.

That afternoon I was not at peace until I sent the text to those who were to receive it. It was a heavy responsibility. The embargo was supposed to last until 7:00 on Sunday morning, but I had not considered something. At midnight on Saturday night, RAI [Radiotelevisione Italiana] put up the front pages of the next morning's newspaper on its website. And naturally *La Verità* had the entire front page dedicated to the pope and McCarrick. Someone pointed this out to our American colleagues, who then ran their articles, anticipating the embargo by several hours.

Why am I giving you these details?

Because from the very first hours and days after publication of the archbishop's testimony, an incredibly vast machine of disinformation and discrediting went to work.

Some concluded that I had written Archbishop Viganò's testimony and, indeed, had practically inspired it. They painted me as a conservative journalist, hostile to the pope, who wanted to put himself in the limelight.

I must say that my opinion of my colleagues—which, I confess, was not terribly high to begin with—tumbled into an immeasurable abyss. Because of ideology, because they were fascinated, because they were paid, because they are in collusion with the institution—these colleagues set out to find the tiniest hair in the egg of Viganò's declarations.

I cannot forget the doubts that were cast everywhere by the pro-Francis[8] press gang about the existence of any steps taken by Pope Benedict XVI against Cardinal McCarrick. It must have been a terrible day for them when Cardinal Ouellet[9] confirmed it in his anti-Viganò tirade (discussed later in these pages). But I am a person capable of rejoicing in every circumstance and able to smile and give thanks.

The focus of Viganò's testimony was—and still is— what I called attention to in my blog *Stilum Curiae* on August 26, 2018, the Sunday morning when *La Verità* published the entire document.

To whit, since 2013, immediately after his election, Pope Francis knew about all the misdeeds of Cardinal Theodore McCarrick. Not only did he choose not to do anything; he even made Cardinal McCarrick his privileged counselor regarding the nomination of bishops and cardinals in the Church in America and for international politics. In effect, the reigning pontiff "covered" for Cardinal McCarrick

---

[8] Jorge Mario Bergoglio (b. 1936) was elevated to the papacy as Pope Francis in 2013.

[9] Cardinal Marc Armand Ouellet (b. 1944): prefect of the Congregation for Bishops.

for five years, all the while knowing that McCarrick had sexually abused dozens of seminarians and young priests.

This is the explosive claim of Archbishop Viganò. Further, in 2013 and in his official capacity, Viganò personally informed the pontiff of McCarrick's misdeeds and did so in response to a request of the pope concerning the situation of this homosexual predator cardinal.

Viganò's claim is contained, along with many other details, in the ten-page document that the archbishop shared with me and on which we worked together.

Among other things, Monsignor Viganò reveals in it that Cardinal McCarrick was previously subjected by Benedict XVI to a punishment analogous to the one he has received in recent weeks, a punishment that, however, Cardinal Wuerl, the archbishop of Washington, never actually applied and that Pope Francis *de facto* canceled from the moment of his election.

Here is what Archbishop Viganò said:

> *The principal reason I am revealing this information now is because of the tragic situation in the Church, which can be repaired only by the full truth, in the same way in which it has been*

gravely wounded by abuse and by intrigues. I am doing it to protect the Church: only the truth can set her free.

The second reason is to unburden my conscience before God of my responsibility as a bishop for the universal Church. I am old, and I want to present myself to God with a clean conscience.

The secrets of the Church, even pontifical secrets, are not taboo. They are instruments for protecting her and her children from her enemies. Secrets should not be used for conspiracies.

The people of God have the right to know the whole truth regarding their pastors. They have the right to be guided by good pastors. In order to be able to trust them and love them, they must know them openly and with transparency. A priest should be a light on a lampstand always and everywhere and for everyone.

The Beginning of the Great Silence

✠ ✠ ✠

✞ ✞ ✞

The pontiff was in Dublin on the Sunday morning of the publication of Viganò's testimony, and that day, on his flight back to Rome, he chose not to say a word. Even unto today, he has not.

Here is the account, according the reputable news site Catholic News Agency:

> "I have read the declaration this morning," [said Pope Francis,] "and I must tell you sincerely, I must say this, to you and to all who are interested: read the declaration attentively and form your own judgment. I will not say another word about this."
>
> [Further, he] said that he believed in the "journalistic capacity to draw one's own conclusions," defining it as an "act of faith." "When some time has passed and you have reached your own conclusions, I will be able to speak. But I would like your professional maturity to do the work for you.

It will be good for you," he said to members of the press.

Asked in a follow-up question when he knew about the accusations of abuse against McCarrick, Pope Francis replied, "This is part of the declaration. Study it and then I will tell you."

We will soon return to the argument, but it seems that the route chosen by the pontiff is an extremely weak way to respond to the legitimate questions that Catholics are raising. In fact, a quick glance through reactions to the attempts at justification adopted on the Web by his communications spin doctor, Antonio Spadaro, S.J.,[10] showed clearly that many people were troubled by it.

Nonetheless, defending Viganò quickly became necessary work, because zealous men (and women) applied themselves fiercely to smearing the figure of the archbishop in every possible way, suggesting motivations and rancor of every sort, all of which were nonexistent. These people count for little, but when the mud hits the fan, it is always a nuisance.

---

[10] Antonio Spadaro, S.J. (b. 1966): editor of the Jesuit-affiliated journal *La Civiltà Cattolica*.

Others with even greater fantasies arrived at the hypothesis that behind Viganò's document there lay hidden the long hand of American bishops who were damaged by the abuse scandals and by the so-called tough policies of Pope Francis.

But the ones who were damaged are all Francis's political creations (McCarrick, Wuerl, Farrell,[11] Tobin[12]) and their friends (Cupich,[13] McElroy,[14] and Sean O'Malley[15])!

---

[11] Cardinal Kevin Joseph Farrell (b. 1947) was auxiliary bishop of Washington, D.C., under Cardinal McCarrick from 2001 to 2006.

[12] Cardinal Joseph William Tobin (b. 1952) was named a cardinal by Pope Francis in November 2016 and installed as cardinal archbishop of Newark in January 2017, a position that Cardinal McCarrick had held some years earlier.

[13] Cardinal Blase Joseph Cupich (b. 1949) was appointed archbishop of Chicago by Pope Francis in 2014 and named a cardinal by Pope Francis in 2016.

[14] Bishop Robert Walter McElroy (b. 1954) was appointed bishop of the Diocese of San Diego by Pope Francis in 2015. In 2016 he was informed of allegations against Cardinal McCarrick but did not act on them, because (he said) he could not determine whether they were credible.

[15] Cardinal Seán Patrick O'Malley, OFM Cap. (b. 1944): archbishop of Boston since 2003. He was sent a letter by a New York priest, Boniface Ramsey, in 2015, detailing sex

What sort of finesse of political calculation could be behind the hypothesis that they would attack Francis?

Finally, we had a female member of the Vatican spin machine who said she "knew" from her sources (we can only imagine who they were) that Viganò was taking psychiatric drugs.

Madam, there are definitely other people inside the Vatican who are taking medicine for their heads! And there are also those who, like several colleagues of mine in foreign press agencies, do not know how to write anything else besides describing Viganò as conservative and strictly anti-gay.

If that were true, would it be a crime? If we consider what homosexuality has done to the American Church, perhaps we would only praise him! But political correctness controls all information, as we know only too well.

☩ ☩ ☩

All these people seemed to forget that there is one and only one point to which there ought to be a response or an explanation—namely: *On June 23, 2013, did Viganò tell the pontiff about McCarrick?*

---

abuse committed by Archbishop McCarrick. He claims never to have seen it himself.

The Beginning of the Great Silence

✠ ✠ ✠

This is the only thing that matters — not whether Viganò
is naturally a son of Hitler or whether he has seven lovers
in Cuba because he fancies the Caribbean.

And this is why the following remarks are particularly valuable. I received them on the day of the "Viganò
bomb" from the blogger Super Ex,[16] who wrote to explain
to us — to my readers and me — why Viganò decided to
speak and to write. Reading his letter made me so happy. I
had not been in touch with Super Ex at all about Viganò,
and thus the article he sent me was a complete surprise.
It made me happy to see that evidently, through means
that had nothing to do with me, other people had come to
similar conclusions about why Archbishop Viganò decided
to take this path, a path on which he would receive only
insults and rebuke.

Judging from the way Super Ex writes, he probably
knows Viganò better than I do, for I have met the archbishop only four times in my life. And so Super Ex can
better explain the "why" that I can only intuit:

---

[16] "Ex" because he is formerly of the *Movimento per la Vita*,
formerly of *Avvenire* — fortunately for him, seeing what
it has now been reduced to — and formerly of many other
things, but still, in fact, not an ex-Catholic.

Let's begin [wrote Super Ex] by clarifying that Carlo
Maria Viganò, the author of the bombshell personal
testimony published [on August 26, 2018] in *La Verità*, is not the same person as Dario Edoardo Viganò,
the monsignor who was in vogue in the gay Vatican
world, until the outbreak of the media scandal [in
April 2018] that did him in and revealed him to the
world as a *pataccaro* [grease spot], one who created
fake news in order to portray Supreme Head Francis
as the continuator of the work of Benedict XVI.[17]

No, Carlo Maria Viganò — whose testimony
Pope Francis did not deny during the plane press
conference — is neither a member of the gay Vatican
lobby nor a manufacturer of fake news who enjoys
papal approval.

Or, to explain it better, this man, Archbishop
Viganò, who, with his denunciation [of Pope Fran-
cis], has everything to lose and nothing to gain,

---

[17] Father Dario Edoardo Viganò (b. 1962): In 2018, while
serving as prefect of the Vatican Secretariat for Communications, Father Viganò inaccurately represented a letter
authored by Pope Emeritus Benedict XVI and provided
journalists with a photograph later shown to be altered,
to imply support by Benedict for views that Benedict
rejected.

formerly had the seal of papal approval at the time of Benedict XVI, who held him in high regard. Then [Secretary of State] Cardinal Tarcisio Bertone[18] (the one who built himself a penthouse using money stolen from Bambino Gesù Hospital), saw fit to remove Viganò, sending him to the USA as nuncio.

We do not need to use our imagination here to see that Providence follows very strange paths — because Bertone thought he would cut off the legs of one of his enemies in his Italian affairs, and yet without intending it, he sent Viganò to the very nation that would become, under Francis's pontificate, a key country for the exposure of evil within the Church.

Viganò was thus removed from his position, unbeknownst to the German pope, who, surrounded by enemies and without practical power, resigned shortly thereafter, basically admitting that he was no longer able to carry out his mission: there were too many Judases surrounding him!

Meanwhile, the new boss, Francis, while placing gay-minded men in key positions everywhere

---

[18] Cardinal Tarcisio Pietro Evasio Bertone (b. 1934) was the Vatican secretary of state from 2006 to 2013.

in Italy, from the aforementioned Dario Edoardo Viganò to Nunzio Galantino [made president of the Italian Bishops' Conference by Francis in 2013] to Vincenzo Paglia [made president of the Pontifical Academy for Life], at the same time launched a war without quarter against the American bishops for their crime of opposing the Obama administration's pro-abortion and pro-gender-ideology agenda.

And thus Pope Francis isolated Cardinal Raymond Burke[19] [removing him from the Congregation of Bishops] and sought to sideline the conservative American Cardinals Timothy Dolan[20] and Daniel DiNardo,[21] turning instead, for a source of new cardinals, to whom?

To the serial abuser Cardinal McCarrick!

One does not need to read the specific testimony of Carlo Maria Viganò to understand this: just scroll

---

[19] Cardinal Raymond Burke (b. 1948) was prefect of the Apostolic Signatura from 2008 to 2014.

[20] Cardinal Timothy Dolan (b. 1950), archbishop of New York since 2009, was president of the United States Conference of Catholic Bishops from 2010 to 2013.

[21] Cardinal Daniel Nicholas DiNardo (b. 1949) has been archbishop of Galveston-Houston since 2006. Since 2016, he has been president of the United States Conference of Catholic Bishops.

through the CVs of the pro-Francis cardinals Wuerl, Cupich, Tobin, etc. Every single one is an intimate friend of McCarrick, and every single one is someone close to the gay lobby!

To be sure, Viganò also offers us further details about the system of cover-up that all of them, McCarrick most of all, profited from under [Secretaries of State] Sodano[22] and Bertone and their associates, even before the flight took off, thanks to Francis.

Viganò does not have an *a priori* objective to bring down Pope Francis: he simply tells the whole truth, including about who was in place [in the system of cover-up] before [Francis]!

Thus, as we have said, Viganò, kicked out of Rome, ended up in the USA, where he fought the internal war within the American episcopate sparked by the new bishops named by Francis as well as by the old progressives who had been disarmed under Benedict XVI.

As he had done in Rome, so, in this case, Viganò followed the correct canonical route and denounced McCarrick to his superiors. He spoke also directly

---

[22] Cardinal Angelo Raffaele Sodano (b. 1927) was the Vatican secretary of state from 1991 to 2006.

with Francis about McCarrick, but without any result.

Then, in 2016, Viganò retired and continued to observe what was happening. On several occasions he spoke with Catholic authorities, who asked him to speak out: "Tell everything, please, for the good of the Church!"

But Viganò had his reservations.... He loved the Church and did not want to hurt her ... and would not act until the time was ripe, until everything that we have seen happen with McCarrick, Maradiaga, and Wuerl, became, at least partially, known publicly and it all ended up in the eye of the hurricane. What did the Supreme Head [Francis] do? He continued to pretend nothing is wrong; worse, he called homosexuality "pedophilia" and once again carefully avoided placing the blame on those who truly are to blame.

Could Viganò, knowing everything, tolerate their continuing to place the blame for the abominations that happened in the USA on a vague "clericalism" in the church in general, on unidentifiable persons?

No. For this reason, for the sake of his love for justice and for the Church, he decided to speak:

the ones who are to blame, the abusers such as Mc-
Carrick, had first and last names, as did those who
covered it all up (from Bertone to Francis).

To speak those names out loud would bring on
insults, slanders, and stomachaches ... but would
there be even one bishop, just one, who would have
the courage to suffer these trials in order to wash
away the disgusting scandals that the faithful were
witnessing?

Behold, Viganò chose to do this.

The true Church thanks him today and will thank
him even more one day in the future, when she will
have completely overcome this long, terrible tragedy,
which has lasted more than forty years but has now
reached its culmination in this grotesque climate
in which, while the world takes in the news of the
abuse by homosexual priests and cardinals against
seminarians and minors, an American Jesuit named
James Martin,[23] protected at the highest levels, attempts doctrinally to justify the obscene behavior of
his American and non-American protectors.

---

[23] Father James J. Martin (b. 1960) is an editor-at-large for
the Jesuit magazine *America* and in 2017 was appointed
by Pope Francis to be a consultant to the Vatican's Secretariat for Communications.

P.S. On January 30, 2012, Vatican journalist Andrea Tornielli, reporting on the strange dismissal of Viganò from his position at the Governorate of Vatican City through the workings of Bertone, remembered the "undeniable results of the moralization and cost-cutting (the Nativity scene in St. Peter's Square, for example, went from costing 550,000 euros to only 300,000). The healing work of Viganò on the [Vatican] budget is a good result not only of his work, but also of his direct superior, Cardinal Giovanni Lajolo, and of the more careful management of the Vatican Museums: all of this work has allowed the Vatican budget to have a surplus of several million euros, whereas previously it had registered a heavy deficit."

Thus, Tornielli, who today is seeking to place Viganò in an ugly light, only a few years ago was praising his character, and he recognized that this praise came also from Benedict XVI: Tornielli wrote of the "full confidence shown by the pontiff toward Viganò, which indicates the recognition of Viganò's merits in the process of rehabilitation [of the governance of the Vatican]."

Tornielli also wondered why, if the accusations made by Viganò in the letters were unfounded, he would then be considered worthy to hold "such a delicate and prestigious position as head of the diplomatic office in Washington, the one responsible for relations with the White House and a close collaborator with the pope in the selection of American bishops, an assignment that requires poise, discretion, and the highest diplomatic skill."

The Mud-Slinging and Disinformation Machine

✠ ✠ ✠

✠ ✠ ✠

As I wrote earlier, the discrediting and disinformation machine went immediately into operation. It was not a new mechanism: the same thing happened at the time of the *dubia* and the dissent against *Amoris Laetitia*.[24] The disinformation machine even went so far as to say that there were people who wrote to Viganò to "convince" him to give his testimony. Servility can lead one to do things that are ridiculous.

The scandal that had been created in America by the release of the Pennsylvania grand jury report of abuse and

---

[24] According to many critics of it, the pope's *Amoris Laetitia* (March 2016) opened the way for civilly divorced and remarried Catholics to receive absolution and Holy Communion while remaining sexually active. On September 19, 2016, four cardinals—the Italian Carlo Caffarra, the American Raymond Burke, and the Germans Walter Brandmüller and Joachim Meisner—formally sought clarification from the pope regarding what appeared to be heretical teaching. As of the date of this writing in 2019, the pope has not responded to their *dubia*.

by the testimony of Viganò stirred up the indignation of American Catholics to such a point that, at the end of August, thousands of Catholics signed an open letter asking the pope to respond to Vigano's denunciation.

Unfortunately, it was not successful.

As the days passed and the only sound that came from the Vatican was silence, not a few people asked why the Holy See was not responding in some way, not only to Vigano's direct accusations claiming that the pontiff had favored and used an abuser cardinal who had been punished by his predecessor, but also to questions directed toward ecclesiastical dignitaries of the Church, both in the recent past and in the present.

Then the Kim Davis case[25] exploded, and the archbishop came out of his place of hiding, this time with a document.

It was September 2015, and Pope Francis was making his first visit to the United States (his first visit ever; he

---

[25] Kimberly Jean Davis (b. 1965) was the county clerk in Kentucky who was jailed for five days in 2015 when she defied a U.S. federal court order to issue marriage licenses to same-sex couples. A few weeks after being released from jail, she met with Pope Francis in Washington, D.C. The Holy See Press Office later noted that the pope met with many others that day and that the meeting was not an endorsement of Davis's actions.

had never set foot there in his entire life). The news of the meeting of the pontiff with Kim Davis came out after his return to Rome. Davis's lawyer, Mathew D. Staver, said that the "private meeting" lasted fifteen minutes, took place in "a separate room" in order to keep it secret, and that those who had organized the meeting insisted that it would be kept secret until after the pope returned to Rome. According to Staver, the pope said that he wanted "to thank Kim Davis for her courage"; he told her to "remain strong"; and he gave her two rosaries. Staver described the meeting as very "cordial" and "warm" and said that Davis and the pope promised to pray for each other.

At the beginning, official Vatican sources refused to comment. Then, on October 2, Father Federico Lombardi[26] issued a communication admitting that there was "a brief meeting" but that it could not be considered to be a form of endorsement for Davis's position, that it was not "an endorsement of her position with all of its particular and complex implications."

Lombardi also said: "The pope met at the Nunciature in Washington with dozens of different people who had

---

[26] Father Federico Lombardi, S.J. (b. 1942), an Italian Catholic priest, was director of the Holy See Press Office from 2006 to 2016.

been invited to the Nunciature to greet him at the time of his departure from Washington for New York City, as happens during all papal trips. We are talking about very short greetings of courtesy for which the pope makes himself available with his characteristic kindness. The only 'audience' which the pope gave at the Nunciature was to one of his former students with his family."

The matter came back front and center after the *New York Times*—which is lined up body and soul with Pope Francis, just as it was with [Hillary] Clinton—published an article about a Chilean victim of sexual abuse, Juan Carlos Cruz, a homosexual, who declared that "the pope recently told him [that] Archbishop Viganò nearly sabotaged the visit" to the United States by inviting Kim Davis, a county clerk from Kentucky who had refused to sign the marriage license of a gay couple. According to the *New York Times*, the pontiff said to Cruz: "I didn't know who that woman was; [Viganò] snuck her in to say hello to me—and of course they made a whole publicity [stunt] out of it.... And I was horrified, and I fired that nuncio," Cruz maintained that the pope had said.[27]

---

[27] "The Man Who Took on Pope Francis: The Story behind the Viganò Letter," *New York Times*, August 28, 2018, https://www.nytimes.com/2018/08/28/world/europe/archbishop-carlo-maria-vigano-pope-francis.html.

Now Viganò has clarified this controversial chapter, and he did so with a written declaration, to which he also added the memorandum on Kim Davis that he sent to the pontiff and to those responsible at the Secretariat of State—the sostituto, Cardinal Giovanni Angelo Becciu, and the secretary for relations with states, Bishop Paul Gallagher—with whom he discussed the affair. Says Archbishop Viganò:

> *At the end of dinner at the Nunciature in Washington on the evening of September 23, 2015, I said to the pope that I needed him to give me half an hour, because I wanted to bring to his attention and eventually seek his approval for a delicate initiative that was easy to carry out. It was the meeting with Davis, the first American citizen to be put in prison for a week because she exercised her right of conscientious objection.*
>
> *At the beginning of our meeting on the evening of September 23, I gave the pope a one-page memorandum that synthesized the Davis case. The pope showed himself immediately favorable to the initiative but added that the meeting would have political ramifications, and he said, "I'm not an expert on these matters, so it's good that you hear Cardinal Parolin's opinion of it."*

Viganò went to the hotel where the Vatican delegation was staying. Parolin[28] was already in bed, so there was a meeting with the sostituto, Monsignor Becciu, and with Monsignor Gallagher. Viganò brought with him two staff members from the Nunciature (one Italian and one Lithuanian).

These five met in a room, and everyone was given a copy of the memorandum that Viganò had already shown the pope. "Monsignor Becciu showed himself immediately favorable to the pope's having a private audience with Davis," Viganò said. Monsignor Gallagher, "although showing that he was in favor of the idea, given the importance of defending the right of conscientious objection," said that they ought to consider whether the legal proceeding against Davis was concluded or still ongoing. Once this problem was resolved, Monsignor Gallagher "gave an unconditional word of approval for the pope to receive Davis," said Viganò.

The next day, after Mass, "I informed the pope of the positive opinion of his two principal collaborators, both of whom would have informed Cardinal Parolin about our meeting," said Viganò. "The pope therefore gave his consent."

Viganò organized things in such a way that Davis arrived at the Nunciature discreetly. "The pope, in the early

---

[28] Cardinal Pietro Parolin (b. 1955) has served as the Vatican secretary of state since 2013.

afternoon of September 24, before departing for New York, entered as planned into the room where Davis and her husband awaited him," Viganò explained. "He embraced her affectionately, thanked her for her courage, and exhorted her to persevere. Davis was very emotional and began to cry." She was taken back to her hotel in a car driven by a gendarme accompanied by an American monsignor from the Nunciature staff.

Then, without consulting the nuncio, the Press Office of the Holy See issued a statement. "Then Father Rosica and Father Lombardi thought of piling on the lies," said Viganò.

One morning not long thereafter, Cardinal Parolin telephoned Viganò: "You must come to Rome immediately because the pope is furious with you." On October 9, Viganò was at Santa Marta.[29] He writes:

> *The pope received me for about an hour, in an affectionate and paternal manner. He apologized immediately for having bothered me by asking me to come to Rome, and he went on in many*

---

[29] Casa Santa Marta, adjacent to St. Peter's Basilica, is the Vatican guesthouse. Pope Francis has made it his residence since his election in March 2013.

words, praising me for how I had organized his visit to the United States, for the incredible welcome that he had received in America, how he had never expected it [to go so well].

To my great surprise, during this whole long meeting, the pope did not mention the audience with Davis even once.

Viganò telephoned Parolin to tell him how the pope had been so well disposed toward him. Parolin responded, "That's impossible, because with me he was furious about you."

In his conclusion, recalling the phrase of Juan Carlos Cruz, Viganò wrote:

One of the two is lying: Is it Cruz or the pope? What is certain is that the pope knew perfectly well who Davis was, and he and his collaborators approved the audience.

If what Monsignor Viganò relates is true — and apparently there is also a document backing up his testimony — the credibility of the official Vatican sources has been destroyed, to say nothing of the sources that are not official but only friends of friends.

The poor Church.

The Vatican Is Silent

✠ ✠ ✠

✠ ✠ ✠

The Vatican remained silent, as did the pope, except to launch veiled insults or to compare those who asked questions to the great accuser or to a wild dog. One person, nonetheless, spoke in defense of Viganò: Romana Vulneratus Curia, a real person whom readers of *Stilum Curiae* know well. Here is what he wrote to me on September 2, 2018:

Dear Tosatti, since I have been out of the country for a while, I had difficulty following the "Viganò denunciation" in its entirety. I have been limited to reading as many newspapers as possible in the last two days and discussing it with a friend who seemed to be well informed. I believe that it may be helpful for the readers of *Stilum Curiae* to read this interpretation of what may have happened, in order perhaps to understand better the disordered interpretations of the motivations that led to the decision of Monsignor Viganò to publish his document as well as the accusations being made against . him by many parties.

But it may also be useful to many holy priests who are not sufficiently informed, to help them to find reasons to doubt their certainty that Viganò was in error in his choice to make his testimony public instead of following other methods — either to go through the hierarchy, or to remain silent, limiting himself simply to praying.

My friend's interpretation, combined with my own, leads me to this synthesis: the reasons for which Monsignor Viganò was punished in past years, by means of three interventions, are the consequence of his responsible behavior in the past.

The punishments that he received in the past are not the cause of his decision now to publish his testimony. It seems that he has decided to go public with his testimony precisely because the problems that he had responsibly denounced in the past have not yet been dealt with and removed.

According to what we read in the newspapers, the three punishments inflicted on him in the past, for which he supposedly nurtured sentiments of revenge, are these:

1. He was relieved of his position as secretary-general of the Governorate of Vatican City and was not named governor, as had been expected.
2. He was not named cardinal, as he had been promised.
3. He was thrown out of the Vatican and sent to be a nuncio.

Well then, it seems that all three of these "punishments," which, according to the commentators hostile to him, are the cause of his desire for revenge, were inflicted on him precisely because, in the past, he did his duty, the same thing he is trying to do today, taking personal responsibility for it.

All the "punishments" are a consequence of his battle against various disorders of a sexual nature (and others) that he discovered and of his consequent denunciations of these disorders (in a formal way through the hierarchy).

It has been explained to us, by those who know him well, that his battle against these disorders began years ago, before his nomination to the Governorate, when he was given the task of investigating these matters in a seminary. There he began to make powerful enemies, who persecuted him, availing themselves of anonymous letters and articles signed with pseudonyms. This continued during his assignment at the Governorate, where he had the courage not to allow himself to be intimidated, and it went on and on.... Don't forget that it was the publication of part of one of his confidential documents written to Benedict XVI that started the first Vatileaks affair.

And at this point, thanks to a very reliable internal source from the Vatican, we are able to affirm—in order to refute once and for all the voices saying that Viganò is vindictive because he did not get a red hat—that Benedict XVI, in the audience he granted Viganò on April 4, 2011, twice offered him the post of prefect of the Congregation for Economic Affairs, at that time held by Cardinal Velasio de Paolis, who was recently named commissioner of the Legionaries of Christ.

According to what has been reported to us in a confidential but reliable manner, the secretary of the Governorate at the time refused the promotion, because he wanted to finish the work of cleaning up the government of the Vatican City State, and he was afraid that if he left, the team he had organized would be dissolved, as, in fact, happened after his departure as nuncio for the United States. This is an unpublished detail of great importance, because it completely neutralizes one of the accusations leveled against the archbishop by the pontifical hagiographers.

But the few times that a written document has emerged from the cloud that envelops the Vatican on Italian mass media, so afraid of disturbing the institution, it has confirmed the claims made by Archbishop Viganò.

For example, a letter from October 2006, scanned and published by Catholic News Service, confirms what Archbishop Viganò claimed in his eleven-page testimony about the cover-up — both in Rome and in the United States — of the complicity that Theodore McCarrick enjoyed as a homosexual predator of seminarians and young priests and about his becoming in the times of Francis the mastermind behind the nomination of bishops and cardinals in the United States.

This letter was written by the secretary of state's sostituto, Leonardo Sandri,[30] who is now cardinal prefect of the Congregation for the Oriental Churches. It refers to a letter written in November 2000 by Father Boniface Ramsey[31] to

---

[30] Cardinal Leonardo Sandri (b. 1943) was substitute for general affairs in the Secretariat of State of the Vatican from 2000 to 2007 and has since been prefect of the Congregation for the Oriental Churches.

[31] Reverend J. Boniface Ramsey, O.P. (b. 1945) was a professor at Immaculate Conception Seminary (which serves the Archdiocese of Newark) from 1987 to 1996; there he learned that the archbishop of Newark, Theodore

Nuncio Gabriel Montalvo,[32] in which he sounded the alarm about the sexual abuse perpetrated by McCarrick. Ramsey declared to Catholic News Service: "I complained about McCarrick's relationships with seminarians and the whole business about sleeping with seminarians and all of that; the whole business that everyone knows about."

Ramsey taught at Immaculate Conception Seminary [in South Orange, New Jersey] from 1986 to 1996. In 2006, Sandri wrote to Ramsey, asking him for information about a priest who was being investigated by the Vatican. Sandri wrote: "I ask with particular reference to the serious matters involving some of the students of Immaculate Conception Seminary, which, in November 2000, you were good enough to bring confidentially to the attention of the then apostolic nuncio in the United States, the late Archbishop Gabriel Montalvo."

McCarrick, was abusing his seminarians at his private beach house. After having spoken to several officials over the years, he wrote about it (in late 2000) to Archbishop Montalvo (then apostolic nuncio to the United States) but received no response. In 2006, he learned from Archbishop Sandri that his letter to Montalvo had nonetheless been forwarded to the Vatican.

[32] Archbishop Gabriel Montalvo Higuera (1930–2006) was apostolic nuncio to the United States from 1998 to 2005.

Strangely, Sandri's message contained no mention of McCarrick. This was because, according to Ramsey, the accusations against the cardinal were "too sensitive." "My letter [of] November 22, 2000, was about McCarrick and it wasn't accusing seminarians of anything; it was accusing McCarrick."

Catholic News Service writes: "The 2006 letter not only confirms past remarks made by Father Ramsey, but also elements of a document written by Archbishop Carlo Maria Viganò, who served as nuncio to the United States from 2011 to 2016."[33]

Thus, at least at this point, even the detractors of the former nuncio are forced to admit that he did not make anything up. And, in fact, the line of conduct of the defenders perched in silence in the papal bunker is being forced to change. This is witnessed by the homosexualist Jesuit James Martin, who writes: "The letter was received in 2000, during the pontificate of St. John Paul II, who, a few months later, made McCarrick a cardinal. He served as

---

[33] Robert Duncan and Junno Arocho Esteves, "Letter Confirms Vatican Officials Knew of McCarrick Allegations in 2000," Catholic News Service, September 7, 2018, https://www.catholicnews.com/services/englishnews/2018/letter-confirms-vatican-officials-knew-of-mccarrick-allegations-in-2000.cfm.

archbishop of Washington, D.C., until 2006, under Benedict XVI. Let us end the unjust blaming of Pope Francis for McCarrick's rise to power."[34]

A few observations.

Concerning neither John Paul II nor Benedict XVI do we have testimony—as we do for Francis—that someone *directly* informed the pope about who McCarrick was and what he was doing. That Francis was told, yes, we have testimony, and he does not want to respond concerning this crucial and central point.

Neither John Paul II nor Benedict XVI (who sanctioned McCarrick, although apparently without much success) was a friend of McCarrick, nor did they benefit (as McCarrick has said) from his work lobbying for them to become pope; nor did they send him around the world as their personal representative; nor did they use him as their preferred counselor for naming bishops and cardinals in the United States. These are all things that Francis has done. Thus, to say that the rationale of James Martin (and of others of the same ilk, Jesuit or not) is lacking, if not simply false, appears more than reasonable.

---

[34] James Martin, SJ (@JamesMartinSJ), Twitter, September 7, 2018, 12:17 p.m., https://twitter.com/JamesMartinSJ/status/1038144354454589440.

Let's recall, one more time, the crux of this story. And that is the testimony made in the first person by Monsignor Viganò about his audience with the pope in June 2013:

> *Immediately after, the pope asked me in a deceitful way: "What is Cardinal McCarrick like?" I answered him with complete frankness and, if you want, with great naiveté: "Holy Father, I don't know if you know Cardinal McCarrick, but if you ask the Congregation for Bishops, there is a dossier this thick about him. He corrupted generations of seminarians and priests, and Pope Benedict ordered him to withdraw to a life of prayer and penance." The pope did not make the slightest comment about those very grave words of mine and did not show any expression of surprise on his face, as if he had already known the matter for some time, and he immediately changed the subject. But then, what was the pope's purpose in asking me that question: "What is Cardinal McCarrick like?" He clearly wanted to find out if I was an ally of McCarrick or not.*

Only in passing, we would like to mention—we will return to the above shortly—that the Church in the United States, just like the Church in Honduras, Chile, and Australia, is about to find itself in the middle of an unprecedented judicial storm, because numerous states have decided to open a chain of investigations on the question of sexual abuse. In the meantime, he has found the time and a way to receive two friends and protégés of ex-cardinal McCarrick—Cupich and Wuerl—and to organize (if the unofficial reports correspond to the truth, as they seem to) a meeting with Cardinal Francesco Coccopalmerio[35] and legal experts in order to study what sanctions could eventually be placed on Archbishop Vigonò.

This, let us tell you, would amount to an error with explosive ramifications: entrusting the punishment for an inconvenient testimony to a cardinal who—the same cardinal claims—had not noticed the strange habits of a secretary who organized homosexual orgies fueled with drugs in a palace of the Holy See right in front of St. Peter's. If we saw this in a movie, we would say that the director was exaggerating, using unrealistic tones and colors in order to discredit the Church.

---

[35] Cardinal Francesco Coccopalmerio (b. 1938) was president of the Pontifical Council for Legislative Texts from 2007 to 2018.

The Strategy of Business as
Usual in the Vatican

✠ ✠ ✠

✠ ✠ ✠

When I bade farewell to Monsignor Viganò at the door of my house on August 22, I asked him: "And now where will you go, Your Excellency?" He answered me: "Look, I am not going to tell you, so that when they ask you, you will not have to lie. But it's better that I disappear for a while."

In fact, on that day, I had not fully reflected on the possible personal consequences for him of his testimony. Little by little, however, my awareness grew, about the strategy going forward of the pontiff and his power base, which was soon confirmed by the nomination of Cardinal Blase Cupich of Chicago as the main cardinal of the group that organized the February 2019 summit on sexual abuse.

You see, Viganò's document raised numerous precise questions. Who favored, covered up, and protected former Cardinal Theodore McCarrick in his career as a homosexual predator? In the document is a list of names, and the last one on the list is the present pontiff, who is said to have been informed of the criminal activity of McCarrick by Nuncio Viganò himself on June 23, 2013; and who is said, notwithstanding this knowledge, to have rehabilitated the cardinal, even making him his counselor and guide for the nomination of bishops and cardinals pleasing to him, what is called "the McCarrick line." This line now includes the archbishop of Newark (Joseph Tobin), the former archbishop of Washington (Donald Wuerl), the present prefect of the Dicastery for the Laity, Family, and Life (Kevin Farrell), the bishop of San Diego (Robert McElroy), the archbishop of Chicago and lead cardinal of the group, Blase Cupich, and others.

☩ ☩ ☩

On his return trip from Dublin, the pontiff declared: "I will not say one word. Read and judge for yourselves." But he did speak — not directly but obliquely, as he usually does, attempting to dignify the absence of an answer that he owes to a precise question by means of the mantle of the silence of Jesus while also insulting — as he is accustomed to do when he finds himself in difficulty — his interlocutors, calling them wild dogs, great accusers (read: demons), and so forth.

In fact, if we consider what happened afterward, we can see that there has been a response, and a dramatic one, at that: the "cover-up" of McCarrick continued, is continuing, and will continue.

How can we understand this?

The pope did not reply directly about the McCarrick case. But Cardinal Óscar Maradiaga[36] spoke. He is the highest-ranking confidant of Pope Francis; he is the confirmed president of the C9 or "Group of Nine";[37] and he was defended by a letter from the pope right smack in the middle of the financial and homosexual scandal that engulfed him and his diocese (on the walls of his cathedral someone wrote "*Cardenal pedofilo*").

In a word, Cardinal Maradiaga's words carry a specific and important weight. Concerning the McCarrick case, he said: "You do not correct a person by transforming something of the private order into a bomb that explodes all over the world and whose fragments cause damage to the faith of so many people. I believe that this case, which is of an administrative nature, should have been made public

---

[36] Cardinal Óscar Andrés Rodríguez Maradiaga, S.D.B. (b. 1942) is a Salesian and a cardinal from Honduras. He is president of Caritas Internationalis and was president of the Latin American Episcopal Conference (CELAM) from 1995 to 1999.

[37] The C9 is a group of nine cardinals from around the world who advise Pope Francis on his most important decisions.

based only on more serene and more objective criteria, not with the negative charge of profoundly bitter expressions."

So, according to the authoritative source closest to the pope, we must wait until the pontiff deigns to let 1.2 billion Catholics know whether, for five years, he covered up and coddled someone whom he knew to be a homosexual predator of priests and seminarians.

It seems that, at Santa Marta, the fact that a cardinal forced and obliged priests and seminarians to have sex with him is considered a matter of the "private order" and that basically this is only an infraction of an administrative nature.

Apply all the tools of the "Me Too" movement to this argument, and imagine the results!

This is merely speculation, you will say, since we do not know whether this is really the position of the leadership of the Vatican.

But there is a confirmation, and it is one of facts, not words. And what a confirmation it is! It is the attitude that the pontiff—and consequently the Vatican—has assumed toward the American bishops who came to the Vatican to ask for a very specific thing: an apostolic investigation,[38] that is, one organized and directed by the Holy See, into the

---

[38] On September 13, 2018, a delegation of the United States Conference of Catholic Bishops, led by its president,

McCarrick case, into his care
given him both in America
he did—including being fe
at Castelli—he flew hig'
until the secular law got in u.
had to wake up, and quickly.

The request for an "apostolic" investigation .
returned to the sender.

And with good reason. In the face of an inquest of this nature, not one door or dossier could remain closed. Evidently neither the pontiff nor the secretary of state—nor any of the cardinals cited by Viganò—desired that those doors and dossiers would be opened.

The cover-up continues.

Thus, dear Catholics, resign yourselves to living with the suspicion, and at this point perhaps with more than just the suspicion, that the present pope covered up and continues to cover up for a homosexual predator cardinal.

This is not a pleasant feeling, because it takes away from the value and credibility of all his words, including those that are healthy and correct. But if logic and facts have a meaning, how can we think otherwise?

Cardinal DiNardo, went to Rome to ask for a Vatican investigation of McCarrick.

...oor, deluded people, or people who are intention-
...g to deceive, can think that bishops' conferences
...ve "a definitive blow" to the problem of abuse, which
...accomplices of the pope's press gang continue to call
...pedophilia" in order not to use the true term: pervasive
clerical homosexuality.

The commentators in America have correctly given a negative judgment to the Roman no to an apostolic investigation of McCarrick.

We close with an observation.

Months have passed since publication of the Viganò testimony, and not one denial of his claims has been registered. The timid attempt made with the Kim Davis case received a devastating response — substantiated with a document — from the former nuncio.

In the meantime, a letter has emerged from Sandri, then sostituto of the secretary of state, that confirms what Viganò declared. None of the persons called into question — not one — has said, "It is not true." The journalists, with rare exceptions, have been expending their energy on the work of personally denigrating Viganò and those who believe his testimony, and they have stopped there. This also reinforces the idea that his testimony is reliable.

Imagine if one or two journalists of the magic circle held in their hands, by chance, one or two cards to play to refute the former nuncio! We must therefore conclude that it is Viganò who has the cards in his hands.

And that they are winning cards.

We are living in truly terrible times for those who still seek to have faith in this Church.

Viganò Returns to Speak:
He Calls Cardinal Ouellet into Question

✠ ✠ ✠

✠ ✠ ✠

At the end of September, Archbishop Viganò returned to make himself heard. He addressed himself directly to Cardinal Marc Ouellet, the prefect of the Congregation for Bishops, calling him into question with an impassioned document, which we publish here in part:

> *Scio Cui Credidi*
> *"I Know in Whom I Have Believed"*
>
> *. . . It has now been nearly a month since I made my testimony, uniquely for the good of the Church, of what happened in my audience with Pope Francis on June 23, 2013, and also in regard to certain matters that it was given me to know in the course of the assignments that were given to me in the Secretariat of State and in Washington, in relation to those who were responsible for having covered up the crimes committed by the former archbishop of the capital city.*

Viganò vs. the Vatican

The decision to reveal these facts was for me the most painful and serious decision that I have ever taken in my entire life. I made it after long reflection and prayer, during months of profound suffering and anguish, during a crescendo of continuous news of terrible events, with thousands of innocent victims destroyed, of vocations and young priestly and religious lives that were shattered. The silence of the pastors who could have been able to remedy it and prevent new victims became ever more indefensible, a devastating crime for the Church. Well aware of the enormous consequences that my testimony would have, because what I was going to reveal involved the Successor of Peter, nevertheless I chose to speak in order to protect the Church, and I declare with a clean conscience before God that my testimony is true. Christ died for the Church, and Peter, Servus servorum Dei, is the first who is called to serve the Bride of Christ.

Certainly, some of the facts that I was going to reveal were protected by the pontifical secret, which I had promised to observe and which I have faithfully observed from the beginning of my service to the Holy See. But the intention of a

secret, *including the pontifical secret, is to protect
the Church from her enemies, not to cover up
and thus become complicit in crimes committed by some of her members. I had become an
involuntary witness to shocking facts, and, as
is written in the* Catechism of the Catholic
Church *(no. 2491), the seal of a secret is not
binding when keeping a secret causes very serious
damage that may be avoided only by the divulging
of the truth. Only the seal of Confession would
have been able to justify my silence.*

*Neither the pope nor any of the cardinals of
Rome have denied the facts that I have affirmed
in my testimony. The saying* "Qui tacet con-
sentit" *[Silence implies consent] surely applies
in this case, because if they wanted to deny my
testimony, all they had to do was say so and
produce the documents in support of their denial. How is it possible not to conclude that the
reason they have not produced any documents is
because they know that the documents confirm
my testimony?*

*The heart of my testimony is that at least
since June 23, 2013, the pope knew from me
how perverse and diabolical McCarrick was,*

*both in his intentions and in his actions, and
instead of taking precautions in his regard, which
every good pastor would have taken, the pope
made McCarrick one of his principal collaborators in the governance of the Church for the
United States, the Curia, and even for China,
a martyr church that we are looking at with great
concern and anxiety at this time.*

*Now the response of the pope to my testi-
mony was: "I will not say one word!"*

*Except that, contradicting himself, he has
compared his silence to that of Jesus at Nazareth
or before Pilate and compared me to the great
accuser, Satan, who sows scandal and division
in the Church, but without ever pronouncing
my name. If he had said, "Viganò has lied," he
would have been contesting my credibility while
attempting to credit his own. But if he did this,
he would have increased the demand on the part
of the People of God and of the world for the
necessary documents to determine which of the
two of us has spoken the truth.*

*Instead, he set into motion a subtle calumny
against me, that calumny that he himself has
often condemned as having the same gravity as*

murder. What's more, he has repeatedly done this in the context of the celebration of the holiest of sacraments, the Eucharist, in which there is no risk of anyone asking him questions, as would happen if he spoke in front of journalists.

When he has spoken to journalists, he has asked them to exercise their profession with maturity and to draw their own conclusions. But how can journalists discover and know the truth if those who are directly implicated refuse to respond to any questions or to release any documents?

The unwillingness of the pope to respond to my accusations and his deafness to the appeals of the faithful to be responsible is absolutely not compatible with his calls for transparency and for the building of bridges rather than walls.

But there is more: the cover-up of McCarrick does not seem to have been an isolated error on the part of the pope. Many other cases have recently been documented by the press, demonstrating that Pope Francis has defended homosexual priests who have committed serious sexual abuses against minors and adults. This includes his role in the case of Father Julio Grassi *in Buenos Aires, his reinstatement of Father Mauro Inzoli after Pope Benedict had removed him from the priestly ministry (up until the moment he was put in jail, and then, at that point, Pope Francis reduced him to the lay state), and his putting an end to the investigation against Cardinal Cormac Murphy-O'Connor for accusations of sexual abuse.*

In the meantime, a delegation of the United States Conference of Catholic Bishops, led by its president, Cardinal DiNardo, went to Rome to ask for a Vatican investigation of McCarrick. Cardinal DiNardo and the other prelates ought to say to the Church in America and to the world: Did the Pope refuse to perform an investigation in the Vatican about the crimes of McCarrick and those responsible for having covered them up? The faithful have the right to know.

I would like to make a special appeal to Cardinal Marc Ouellet, because, as nuncio, I often worked in concert with him and I always had great esteem and affection for him. He will recall how, when my mission in Washington was almost over, he hosted me one evening at his apartment in Rome for a long conversation. At the beginning of the pontificate of Pope Francis he had maintained his dignity, as he had demonstrated courage when he was archbishop of Quebec.

Later, however, when his work as prefect of the Congregation for Bishops was virtually compromised because the presentation of episcopal nominations passed directly to the pope by way of two homosexual "friends" of his dicastery, bypassing the cardinal, he yielded.

A long article that he wrote in L'Osservatore Romano *in which he lined up in favor of the most controversial aspects of* Amoris Laetitia *represented his surrender. Your Eminence, before I left for Washington, you spoke to me about the sanctions that Pope Benedict had established regarding McCarrick. You have at your disposal all the most important documents incriminating McCarrick and many in the Curia who had covered him up. Your Eminence, I warmly ask you to choose to render testimony to the truth!*

Finally, I want to encourage you, dear faithful brothers and sisters in Christ: Do not ever become discouraged! Make your own the act of faith and complete trust in Christ Jesus our Savior made by Saint Paul in his Second Letter to Timothy, Scio Cui Credidi, which I chose as my episcopal motto. This is a time of penance, of conversion, of grace, to prepare the Church, the Bride of the Lamb, to be ready to fight and win, in union with Mary, the battle against the infernal dragon.

"Scio Cui credidi" (2 Tim 1:12).

In You, Jesus, my only Savior, I place all my trust.

Monsignor Viganò then recalled the Gospel passage about the storm that raged while Jesus slept aboard the boat:

> *The scene is relevant more than ever, because it portrays the tremendous storm that the Church is passing through at this very moment, but with one essential difference: the Successor of Peter not only does not see the Lord in full control of the boat; he does not even intend to wake up Jesus sleeping in the bow. Has Christ perhaps become invisible to His Vicar? Is he perhaps tempted to improvise as a substitute for our one Master and Lord?*

The Lord is in full command of the boat!
May Christ the Truth always be the Light
along our path!

September 29, 2018
Feast of Saint Michael the Archangel

✠ ✠ ✠

Naturally, the Pope Francis press gang immediately laid into the letter of the former nuncio to America. "Viganò: New Statement with the Same Accusations and the Same Omissions" was the headline on a para-Vatican website about this new accurate testimony and request for *parrhesia* (frankness), transparency, clarity, and dialogue. That article conveniently forgot, however, that the most sensational omission of all can unfortunately be attributed to the pope, who, months later, has still made no response to what Viganò declares is "the heart of my testimony." And that is that

> *at least since June 23, 2013, the pope knew from*
> *me how perverse and diabolical McCarrick was,*
> *both in his intentions and in his actions, and in-*
> *stead of taking precautions in his regard, which*
> *every good pastor would have taken, the pope*
> *made McCarrick one of his principal collabo-*
> *rators in the governance of the Church for the*

Viganò vs. the Vatican

United States, the Curia, and even for China, a
martyr church that we are looking at with great
concern and anxiety at this time."

Is this true or not true?

The answer to this crucial question posed by Viganò has been evaded to this day, even though it could be answered in seconds. But they are heavy seconds, judging by the expression of the pontiff when Cindy Wooden of Catholic News Service tried to ask him something about McCarrick during the flight back from Tallinn, Estonia, on September 25, 2018.

There are two points in the new testimony of Viganò that seem to me to be pregnant. The first is when he confesses that deciding to speak was the most difficult decision of his life. And the second is this phrase: "I declare with a clear conscience before God that my testimony is true." We would like to hear from the pope a testimony about these facts and hear him pronounce the same formula.

The Holy See and
Cardinal Ouellet Speak

✠ ✠ ✠

✠ ✠ ✠

Finally, on October 6, the Holy See broke the silence, with a statement of which we repeat the essential part here:

> After the publication of the accusations regarding the conduct of Archbishop Theodore Edgar McCarrick, the Holy Father Pope Francis, aware of and concerned by the confusion that these accusations are causing in the minds of the faithful, has established that the following be communicated:
>
> In September 2017, the Archdiocese of New York notified the Holy See that a man had accused former Cardinal McCarrick of having abused him in the 1970s. The Holy Father ordered a thorough preliminary investigation into this, which was carried out by the Archdiocese of New York, at the conclusion of which the relevant documentation was forwarded to the Congregation for the Doctrine of the Faith. In the meantime, because

grave indications emerged during the investigation, the Holy Father accepted the resignation of Archbishop McCarrick from the College of Cardinals, prohibiting him by order from exercising public ministry, and obliging him to lead a life of prayer and penance.

The Holy See will, in due course, make known the conclusions of the matter regarding Archbishop McCarrick. Moreover, with reference to other accusations brought against Archbishop McCarrick, the Holy Father has decided that information gathered during the preliminary investigation be combined with a further thorough study of the entire documentation present in the Archives of the Dicasteries and Offices of the Holy See regarding the former Cardinal McCarrick, in order to ascertain all the relevant facts, to place them in their historical context and to evaluate them objectively.

The Holy See is conscious that, from the examination of the facts and of the circumstances, it may emerge that choices were made that would not be consonant with a contemporary approach to such issues. However, as Pope Francis has said: "We will follow the path of truth wherever it may lead" (Philadelphia, 27 September 2015). Both abuse and its cover-up can no longer be tolerated and a different treatment for Bishops who have committed or covered up abuse, in fact, represents a form of clericalism that is no longer acceptable.

The Holy Father Pope Francis renews his pressing invitation to unite forces to fight against the grave scourge of abuse within and beyond the Church, and to prevent such crimes from being committed in the future, to the harm of the most innocent and most vulnerable in society. As previously made known, the Holy Father has convened a meeting of the Presidents of the Bishops' Conferences from around the world for next February [2019], while the words of his recent Letter to the People of God still resonate: "The only way that we have to respond to this evil that has darkened so many lives is to experience it as a task for all of us as the People of God. This awareness of being part of a people and a shared history will enable us to acknowledge our past sins and mistakes with a penitential openness that can allow us to be renewed from within" (20 August 2018).[39]

---

[39] Holy See Press Office Communiqué, June 10, 2018, Vatican website.

Viganò vs. the Vatican

✝ ✝ ✝

Have you read it all? Good.

So: it took more than the biblical forty days since the night of August 25–26, when the Viganò bomb exploded, for the Vatican to find the strength, the breath, and the energy necessary to say something.

Not to Viganò, who is never mentioned.

To say what, then?

Essentially: we will investigate, and when God wills it, we will tell you what we have found out.

The Holy See said that the investigation will be done "in order to ascertain all the relevant facts, to place them in their historical context and to evaluate them objectively." What does this mean? I do not understand, but I suspect it is a form of preparing us for leniency.

What follows that passage is even worse:

The Holy See is conscious that, from the examination of the facts and of the circumstances, it may emerge that choices were made that would not be consonant with a contemporary approach to such issues. However, as Pope Francis has said: "We will follow the path of truth wherever it may lead" (Philadelphia, 27 September 2015). Both abuse and its cover-up can no longer be tolerated and a different treatment for Bishops who have committed or covered up abuse, in fact represents a form of clericalism that is no longer acceptable.

A contemporary approach?

And what was the noncontemporary approach (that is, of twenty or thirty years ago)? Was a cardinal's sodomizing seminarians and young priests not as serious in the 1980s and 1990s as it is today? So now, if we judge harshly, would we be guilty of historical anachronism?

And continuing: Were abuses and cover-ups tolerated twenty years ago? And what type of clericalism was acceptable then but is not acceptable now? Do they realize what they write in the Secretariat of State or in Santa Marta?

The statement speaks only of McCarrick. But there is an important detail missing, for which there is no need to go fetching archives and folders. What is missing is the earlier answer of the pope to Carlo Maria Viganò's personal report to him. Here it is again:

> *Immediately after, the pope asked me in a deceitful way: "What is Cardinal McCarrick like?" I answered him with complete frankness and, if you want, with great naiveté: "Holy Father, I don't know if you know Cardinal McCarrick, but if you ask the Congregation for Bishops,*

there is a dossier this thick about him. He corrupted generations of seminarians and priests, and Pope Benedict ordered him to withdraw to a life of prayer and penance." The pope did not make the slightest comment about those very grave words of mine and did not show any expression of surprise on his face, as if he had already known the matter for some time, and he immediately changed the subject. But then, what was the pope's purpose in asking me the question: "What is Cardinal McCarrick like?" He clearly wanted to find out if I was an ally of McCarrick or not.

It will be interesting to find out if they really follow "the path of truth wherever it may lead." We shall see.

On October 7, 2018, the day after the Vatican response, the one who had been directly called into question by Viganò, the prefect for the Congregation of Bishops, Cardinal Marc Ouellet, also decided, after an audience with Pope Francis, to respond:

Dear brother Carlo Maria Viganò,

In your last message to the media, in which you denounce Pope Francis and the Roman Curia, you exhorted me to tell the truth about the facts that you interpret as an endemic corruption that has invaded the hierarchy of the Church even to its highest level. With the necessary pontifical permission, I offer here my personal testimony as prefect of the Congregation for Bishops about matters concerning the archbishop emeritus of Washington, Theodore McCarrick, and his presumed links to Pope Francis, which constitute the object of your sensational public denunciation as well as your demand that the Holy Father resign. I write my testimony based on my personal contacts and on documents in the archives of the Congregation, currently the object of a study in order to shed light on this sad case....

Let's get to the facts. You say that you informed Pope Francis on June 23, 2013, about the McCarrick case in an audience that he granted you, as he did to many other pontifical representatives whom he met for the first time that day. I imagine there must have been an enormous amount of verbal and written information that he had to gather on that occasion about many persons and situations. I strongly doubt that McCarrick interested him as much as you would like to believe, given the fact that by then McCarrick was an eighty-two-year-old archbishop emeritus who had been retired for seven years. Moreover, the written instructions prepared for you by the Congregation for Bishops at the beginning of your service in 2011 did not say anything about McCarrick, except for what I said to you verbally about his situation as bishop emeritus, that he ought to obey certain conditions and restrictions as a result of some rumors about his behavior in the past.

Since June 30, 2010, when I became prefect of this Congregation, I never presented the McCarrick case in an audience with either Pope Benedict XVI or to Pope Francis, until recently, after McCarrick's dismissal from the College of Cardinals. The former cardinal, who retired in May 2006, was strongly exhorted not to travel or to make public appearances, in order not to provoke new rumors in his regard. It is false to present the measures taken in his regard as "sanctions" decreed by Pope Benedict XVI and then annulled by Pope Francis. After re-examining the archives, I observe that there are no documents in this regard signed by either pope, and there are no audience notes from my predecessor, Cardinal Giovanni-Battista Re, which would have mandated an obligation on the part of Archbishop emeritus McCarrick to silence and a private life with the rigor of canonical penalties. The reason is that, at that time, unlike today, there were no sufficient proofs of his presumed culpability. Thus, the position of the Congregation was inspired by prudence, and the letters from my predecessor and my own letters reiterated, first through the apostolic nuncio Pietro Sambi and then through you, the exhortation to a discreet way of life of prayer and penance, for his own good and for the good of the Church. His case would have been the object of new disciplinary measures if the Nunciature in Washington, or any other source, had provided us recent and definitive information about his behavior. I hope, as do many people, that, out of respect for the victims and as justice requires, the investigation currently underway in the United States and in the Roman Curia will finally offer us a critical and comprehensive vision of the procedures and the circumstances of this painful case, so that things of this nature may not be repeated in the future....

Dear pontifical representative emeritus, I tell you frankly that to accuse Pope Francis of having covered up, with full knowledge of the matter, an alleged sexual predator and of thus being an accomplice in the corruption that is rampant in the Church, to the point of feeling him unworthy to continue to carry out his reform as the first shepherd of the Church, appears to me incredible and far-fetched from all points of view. I am not able to understand how you could have allowed yourself to be convinced of this monstrous accusation that does not stand on its own legs.

Francis had nothing to do with McCarrick's promotions to New York, Metuchen, Newark, and Washington. He stripped him of the dignity of being a cardinal as soon as there was a credible accusation of abuse of a minor. I never heard Pope Francis allude to this so-called great adviser for episcopal nominations in America, although he does not hide the trust that he places in certain prelates.

I intuit that those prelates are not of your preference or the preference of your friends who support your interpretation of the facts. I think it is abhorrent, however, for you to use the sensational scandal of sexual abuse in the United States to inflict an unmerited and unheard-of blow against the moral authority of your superior, the supreme pontiff.

I have the privilege of having long meetings with Pope Francis every week to discuss the appointment of bishops and the problems that affect their governance. I know very well how he deals with persons and problems: with much charity, mercy, attention, and seriousness, as you yourself have also experienced. Reading the conclusion of your last message, which appeared to be very spiritual, making fun of the Holy Father and casting a doubt on his faith, it seemed to me to be truly too sarcastic, and even blasphemous! That cannot come from the Spirit of God....

If the pope were not a man of prayer; if he were attached to money; if he favored riches to the detriment of the poor; if he did not demonstrate a tireless energy to welcome all those who are miserable and to give them the generous comfort of his words and actions; if he did not multiply all the possible means to announce and to communicate the joy of the Gospel to every man and woman in the Church and beyond her visible horizons; if he did not lend a hand to the families, to the abandoned elderly, to the sick in body and soul, and, above all, to the youth in their search for happiness, one could prefer someone else, according to you, with a different political or diplomatic approach. But I, who have been able to know him well, cannot call into question his personal integrity, his consecration to the mission and, above all, the charisma and peace he enjoys through the grace of God and the power of the Risen One.

Viganò vs. the Vatican

In response to your attack, which is unjust and unjustified by the facts, dear Viganò, I can only conclude that the accusation is a political plot that lacks any real basis that could incriminate the pope and that profoundly wounds the communion of the Church. May it please God that this injustice may be rapidly repaired and that Pope Francis may continue to be recognized for what he is: a distinguished shepherd, a compassionate and firm father, a prophetic charism for the Church and for the world. May he continue with joy and full confidence his missionary reform, comforted by the prayer of the people of God and by the renewed solidarity of the whole Church, together with Mary, Queen of the Holy Rosary!

Marc Cardinal Ouellet
Prefect of the Congregation for Bishops
Feast of Our Lady of the Holy Rosary
October 7, 2018

✠ ✠ ✠

Some observations: Cardinal Ouellet was received by the pontiff immediately after the second Viganò document appeared, inviting him to tell the truth. We may reasonably think that the response of Ouellet takes into account the thought of the pope.

There are two important points: the conversation of June 23, 2013, in which Viganò supposedly told the pontiff who McCarrick was, and whether there existed sanctions imposed by Benedict XVI.

Ouellet does not deny that the audience of 2013 took place, and he does not deny that the two men spoke of McCarrick:

> I imagine there must have been an enormous amount of verbal and written information that he had to gather on that occasion about so many persons and situations. I strongly doubt that McCarrick interested him as much as you would like to believe, given the fact that by then he was an eighty-two-year-old archbishop emeritus who had been retired for seven years.

This would all sound reasonable and credible, were it not for one fact: it was the pope who asked Viganò about McCarrick, a sign that this matter was of interest to him. And the response of Viganò was of such dramatic gravity and seriousness that we cannot believe that it just slipped through the pope's memory like water. This is an attempt by Ouellet to minimize the importance of a central event, but it doesn't really work. It also indirectly confirms the accuracy of Viganò's account.

Next, the sanctions.

Ouellet met Viganò before he left for the United States as nuncio. Now he writes:

> Moreover, the written instructions prepared for you by the Congregation for Bishops at the beginning of your service in 2011 did not say anything about Mc-Carrick, except for what I said to you verbally about his situation as bishop emeritus, that he ought to obey certain conditions and restrictions as a result of some rumors about his behavior in the past. Since June 30, 2010, when I became prefect of this Congregation, I never presented the McCarrick case in an audience with either Pope Benedict XVI or to Pope Francis, until recently, after his dismissal from the College of Cardinals. The former cardinal, who retired in May 2006, was strongly exhorted not to travel or to make public appearances, in order not to provoke new rumors in his regard. It is false to present the measures taken in his regard as "sanctions" decreed by Pope Benedict XVI and then annulled by Pope Francis.

Ouellet thus admits—and this is the first official confirmation of this fact—that McCarrick was placed under restrictions by Benedict XVI. You may call them what you wish—sanctions, or restrictions, or conditions not written but verbal—but the result does not change. He was not supposed to travel, nor was he to appear in public.

Ouellet writes further that "letters from my predecessor and my own letters reiterated, first through the apostolic nuncio Pietro Sambi and then through you, the exhortation to a discreet way of life of prayer and penance, for his own good and for the good of the Church."

The first thing McCarrick said to Viganò upon meeting him after the March 2013 papal election was that he had spoken with the pope and that the pope was sending him to China. The record of the following years demonstrates that the "sanctions" for McCarrick no longer existed. And thus, Pope Francis modified the "conditions" that had been fixed by Benedict XVI.

Ouellet writes that it is false to present the measures communicated to McCarrick as sanctions. But which is falser: to present these "exhortations" as sanctions or to try to make people believe that Francis did not have a different attitude toward McCarrick than Benedict XVI did?

In conclusion, it seems to me that, apart from the side dishes of the reprimand, the praises of the Pope, and the exhortation to repent and return to the fold, the meat of the Ouellet document confirms the testimony of Viganò.

The Third Testimony of Viganò:
A Cry from the Heart

✠ ✠ ✠

✠ ✠ ✠

Naturally, Archbishop Viganò, the consummate diplomat, did not shy away from the opportunity offered by his interlocutor to reaffirm the veracity of his testimony. He did so on October 19, 2018. It is the strongest document, the most important, and—we are not afraid to use this term—the most historic of this entire dramatic affair. For this reason, we publish it here in its entirety.

Memorial of the North American Martyrs

The decision to testify to the corruption in the hierarchy of the Catholic Church was a painful one for me, and it remains so. But I am an old man, one who knows that soon he must give an account to the Judge of his actions and omissions, one who fears Him who can throw body and soul into hell, the Judge who, although He is infinitely merciful, "will render to each one according to his merits an eternal reward or punishment"

(Act of Faith). Anticipating the terrible question from that Judge — "How were you able, you who knew the truth, to remain silent in the midst of such falsehood and depravity?" — what response would I have been able to give?

I spoke in full knowledge that my testimony would provoke alarm and dismay among many eminent persons: ecclesiastics, brother bishops, colleagues with whom I worked and prayed. I knew that many would feel themselves wounded and betrayed. I foresaw that some of them would, in their turn, accuse me and would discuss my intentions. And, the most painful thing of all, I knew that many innocent faithful people would be confused and disturbed by the spectacle of a bishop accusing his brothers and superiors of misdeeds, sexual sins, and grave negligence toward their duty. Yet I believed that my continued silence would have placed many souls in danger, and it would have certainly condemned my own. Although I had reported the aberrant actions of McCarrick many times to my superiors, and even to the pope himself, I could have publicly spoken earlier about the truth that I knew. If I bear responsibility for this delay, I am sorry. This delay was due to the gravity of the decision I was taking and the long battle within my conscience.

I have been accused of creating confusion and division within the Church. This accusation can be credible only for those who believe that such confusion and division was nonexistent prior to August 2018. Many a dispassionate observer, however, would have been able clearly to see the prolonged and significant presence of divisions, something that is inevitable when the Successor of Peter refuses to exercise his principal mission, which is to confirm the brethren in faith and sound morals. When he has then aggravated the crisis by giving contradictory messages or making ambiguous statements, the confusion has only worsened.

Therefore I spoke, because it is the conspiracy of silence that has caused and continues to cause enormous damage to the Church, to so many innocent souls, to young priestly vocations, and to the faithful in general. In view of my decision, which I made in conscience before God, I willingly accept every fraternal correction, counsel, recommendation, and invitation to progress in my life of faith and love for Christ, the Church, and the pope.

Permit me to recall once again the principal points of my testimony.

- *In November 2000, the nuncio to the United States, Archbishop Montalvo, informed the Holy See of the homosexual behavior of Cardinal McCarrick with priests and seminarians.*

- *In December 2006, the new nuncio, Archbishop Pietro Sambi, informed the Holy See of the homosexual behavior of Cardinal McCarrick with another priest.*

- *In December 2006, I also wrote a memorandum to Secretary of State Cardinal Bertone, which I personally gave to the sostituto for general affairs, Archbishop Leonardo Sandri, asking the pope to take extraordinary disciplinary measures against McCarrick in order to prevent future crimes and scandals. This memorandum received no response.*

- *In April 2008, an open letter to Pope Benedict by Richard Sipe was transmitted to the prefect of the Congregation for the Doctrine of the Faith, Cardinal Levada, and to the secretary of state, Cardinal Bertone, which* contained further accusations of McCarrick going to bed with seminarians and priests. It was sent to me a month later.

• In May 2008, I personally presented a second memorandum to the then-sostituto for general affairs, Archbishop Fernando Filoni, referring to the accusations against McCarrick and asking for sanctions against him. This second memorandum also received no response.

• In 2009 or 2010, I learned from Cardinal Re, prefect of the Congregation for Bishops, that Pope Benedict had ordered McCarrick to cease public ministry and to begin a life of prayer and penance. Nuncio Sambi communicated the orders of the pope to McCarrick, raising his voice so much that it was heard in the corridors of the Nunciature.

• In November 2011, Cardinal Ouellet, the new prefect of the Congregation for Bishops, reconfirmed to me, the new nuncio to the United States, the restrictions placed on McCarrick by the pope, and I personally communicated them to McCarrick face-to-face.

• On June 21, 2013, at the end of a meeting of the nuncios in the Vatican, Pope Francis

*reproved me about the American episcopate,
using words that were difficult to understand.*

- *On June 23, 2013, I met Pope Francis personally in a private audience in his apartment in order to clarify things, and the pope asked me, "What is Cardinal McCarrick like?" —words that I can interpret only as a false curiosity to discover whether I was allied with McCarrick or not. I told him that McCarrick had sexually corrupted generations of priests and seminarians and that Pope Benedict had ordered him to dedicate himself solely to a life of prayer and penance.*

McCarrick however continued to enjoy special consideration from Pope Francis, who also entrusted to him new important responsibilities and missions.

McCarrick formed part of a network of bishops favorable to homosexuality, who, enjoying the favor of the pope, promoted episcopal nominations in order to protect themselves from justice and reinforce homosexuality in the hierarchy and in the Church in general. Pope Francis himself seems to be involved in the spread of this corruption or at least aware of what they do and is gravely responsible because he does not oppose it or seek to eradicate it.

I have invoked God as a witness of the truth of these my affirmations, and none of them have been denied. Cardinal Ouellet has written reproving me for my temerity in having broken the silence and making grave accusations against my brothers and superiors, but, in truth, his reproof confirms me in my decision and confirms the truth of what I have affirmed, point by point and in toto.

* *Cardinal Ouellet admits to having spoken to me about the McCarrick situation before I left for Washington to begin my assignment as nuncio.*
* *Cardinal Ouellet admits to having communicated with me in writing about the conditions and restrictions placed on McCarrick by Pope Benedict.*
* *Cardinal Ouellet admits that these restrictions forbade McCarrick from traveling and appearing in public.*
* *Cardinal Ouellet admits that the Congregation for Bishops, in writing, first through Nuncio Sambi and then through me, ordered*

McCarrick to lead a life of prayer and penance.

What does Cardinal Ouellet contest in my testimony?

- *Cardinal Ouellet contests the possibility that Pope Francis would have been able to recall important information about McCarrick on a day on which he had met dozens of nuncios and gave to each one only a few moments of attention. But this is not what I testified happened. I testified that, in a second private meeting, I informed the pope, responding to his question about Theodore McCarrick, then cardinal archbishop of Washington, a prominent figure in the Church in the United States, and told the pope that McCarrick had sexually corrupted his seminarians and priests. No pope could forget this.*

- *Cardinal Ouellet contests the existence in his archives of letters signed by Pope Benedict or Pope Francis regarding the sanctions on McCarrick. But this is not what I testified. I testified that he had in his archives key documents — regardless of their provenance — incriminating McCarrick and related to the provisions taken in his regard, and other proofs of the cover-up regarding his situation. And I still confirm this.*

- *Cardinal Ouellet contests the existence in his archives of his predecessor, Cardinal Re, of "audience notes" that placed the mentioned restrictions on McCarrick. But this is not what I testified. I testified that there are other documents: for example, a note of Cardinal Re that is not from an audience with the Holy Father or signed by the secretary of state or the sostituto.*

- *Cardinal Ouellet contests that it is false to present the measures taken against McCarrick as "sanctions" decreed by Pope Benedict and then annulled by Pope Francis. True. They were not technically "sanctions"; they were provisions, "conditions and restrictions." To analyze whether they were sanctions or provisions or something else is pure legalism. From a pastoral point of view, it is the same thing.*

In brief, Cardinal Ouellet admits the important affirmations that I made and still make, and he contests the affirmations that I do not and never have made.

Viganò vs. the Vatican

There is one point on which I must absolutely deny what Cardinal Ouellet writes. The cardinal affirms that the Holy See knew only about simple "rumors" about McCarrick, which were not enough to be the basis for taking disciplinary measures against McCarrick.

I affirm instead that the Holy See knew from a multiplicity of concrete facts and was in possession of documents that proved it, but, notwithstanding this, the responsible persons preferred not to intervene or were prevented from doing so. The compensation given to the victims of McCarrick's sexual abuse by the Archdiocese of Newark and the Diocese of Metuchen; the letters of Father Ramsey, of Nuncios Montalvo in 2000 and Sambi in 2006, of Doctor Sipe in 2008; my two memoranda to my superiors in the Secretariat of State that described in detail the concrete accusations against McCarrick — are these only rumors?

They are official correspondence, not gossip from the sacristy. The crimes denounced were very grave. There were also crimes of the absolution of accomplices in repugnant acts, followed by the sacrilegious celebration of Mass.

The Third Testimony of Viganò

These documents specify the identity of the perpetrators, the identity of their protectors, and the chronological sequence of the facts. They are kept in the appropriate archives; no extraordinary investigation is needed to recover them.

In the accusations made publicly against me, I have noted two omissions, two dramatic silences. The first silence is about the victims. The second is about the root cause of so many victims, which is the role of homosexuality in the corruption of the priesthood and the hierarchy.

Regarding the first silence, it is shocking that, amid so many scandals and so much indignation, there is so little consideration for those who were victims of sexual predators who were ordained ministers of the gospel. It is not a question of settling accounts or about ecclesiastical careers. It is not a question of how historians of the Church may evaluate this or that papacy. It is about souls! Many souls have been placed (and are still) in danger [of losing] their eternal salvation.

Regarding the second silence, this very grave crisis cannot be properly faced and resolved until we call things by their true names. This is a crisis caused by the scourge of homosexuality: in those who practice it, in its politics, and in its resistance to being corrected.

It is not an exaggeration to say that homosexuality has become a plague in the clergy that can be eradicated only with spiritual weapons. It is an enormous hypocrisy to condemn abuse, to speak of tears for the victims, and yet refuse to denounce the principal cause of so much sexual abuse: homosexuality.

It is hypocrisy to refuse to admit that this plague is caused by a grave crisis in the spiritual life of the clergy and fail to take the steps necessary to remedy it.

Undoubtedly there are also philandering clergy, and these offenses also create grave damage to the souls of those who commit them, to the Church, and to the souls of those whom they corrupt. But these infidelities to priestly celibacy are usually limited to the individuals immediately involved; they do not tend by themselves to lead to promotion, to the spread of similar behavior, to the cover-up of similar misdeeds; whereas there is overwhelming evidence that the plague of homosexuality in the priesthood is endemic, is spread *through contagion, and has deep roots that are difficult to eradicate.*

It is established that homosexual predators exploit their clerical privilege to their advantage. But to claim that the crisis itself is one of clericalism is pure sophistry. To do so is to pretend that a means, an instrument, is the principle cause.

Denouncing homosexual corruption and the moral cowardice that allows it to grow does not meet with universal approval these days, not even at the highest levels of the Church. It does not surprise me that in calling attention to these scourges, I have been accused of disloyalty toward the Holy Father and of fomenting an open and scandalous rebellion.

But rebellion would imply encouraging others to overthrow the papacy. I am not calling for anything of that sort. I pray every day for Pope Francis more than I ever have for any other pope. I ask — indeed, I implore — that the Holy Father will face the commitments he has made. By agreeing to become a Successor of Peter, he has taken on himself the mission of confirming his brethren and the responsibility of guiding all

*souls to follow Christ in the spiritual battle along
the Way of the Cross.*

*May he admit his errors, repent, and show
that he wants to follow the mandate given to
Peter, and once he has amended his ways, may
he confirm his brothers (Luke 22:32).*

*In conclusion, I desire to repeat my appeal to
my brother bishops and priests who know that my
affirmations are true and who can testify to their
truth, or who have access to the documents that
are able to resolve this situation beyond any doubt.*

You also are now faced with a choice.

*You can choose to retreat from the battle,
to continue in the conspiracy of silence, and to
turn your face away from the advance of corruption. You can invent excuses, compromises, and
justifications that put off the day of reckoning.
You can console yourself with falsehood and the
illusion that it will be easier to speak the truth
tomorrow, and then again the next day.*

Or you can choose to speak.

*You can have faith in the One who has
said, "The truth will set you free." I do not
say that it will be easy to decide between silence
and speaking. I exhort you to consider which*

choice — on your deathbed and then before the Just Judge — you will not regret having made.

+ Carlo Maria Viganò
Titular Archbishop of Ulpiana
Apostolic Nuncio
October 19, 2018

The Silence of the Pope:
A Wound for the Church

✠ ✠ ✠

✠ ✠ ✠

The nonresponse of the pope to Viganò represents, in my view, a wound to his credibility as a human being and as a spiritual leader, and in the final analysis, a wound also to his mission.

A similar opinion has now been expressed — for the first time against Pope Francis — in international headlines in journals, including the *New York Times*, the *Frankfurter Allgemeine*, *Der Spiegel*, the *Wall Street Journal*, the *Catholic Herald*, and still others. Christian Geyer wrote for the *Frankfurter*:

Not even Francis ("I will not say one word") could rely on his wisdom and his lofty vision to justify the silence he has chosen, unless he wants to eliminate the principle of personal responsibility in his Church and sweep away the credibility of his magisterial authority.

Yet his refusal to answer unpleasant questions during his press conference on the [September 25,

2018,] flight returning from the Baltic States follows this model. At first, the questions relating to
Viganò were postponed until later; then they were
not permitted at all. ("They told me that dinner is
ready and the flight is short.")

It is no surprise, even if it is disgusting, that our
German bishops have felt the need to follow the
example of the Pope.

Harsh, right?

To say nothing of *Der Spiegel*, which ran an insert of
several pages on the question of abuse that had on its cover
a photograph of Pope Francis in a shadow, surmounted
by the words "You shall not bear false witness." Even the
Catholic journal *Herder Korrespondenz* criticized the choice
of silence being used by the Vatican authorities.

On October 12, 2018, after a petition calling for his resignation received thousands of signatures, Cardinal Wuerl
resigned. He was the archbishop of Washington, the man
who was supposed to watch over McCarrick but did not do so.

Once again, ambiguity reigned. Although, according
to the Pennsylvania grand jury report, Wuerl was heavily
implicated in the cover-up of abuse, the pope wrote a letter praising Wuerl and named him apostolic administrator
of the Archdiocese of Washington, thereby practically

allowing him to remain in power with no time limit. These moves by the pope have a "business as usual" feel to them and have now alienated even the sympathies of the American progressivist media.

✠ ✠ ✠

I said earlier that it seems to me that the third testimony of Archbishop Viganò is perhaps the strongest, most pregnant document in this whole affair. This is not only my opinion. In the *National Catholic Register*, Monsignor Charles Pope expressed a similar view:

As I finished reading Archbishop Carlo Maria Viganò's third letter, I had an immediate sense that I had just read something that is destined to be one of the great pastoral and literary moments of the Church's history. There was an air of greatness about it that I cannot fully describe. I was stunned at its soteriological quality—at its stirring and yet stark reminder of our own judgment day. In effect he reminded us that this is more than a quibble over terminology or who wins on this or that point, or who is respectful enough of whom. This is about the salvation of souls, including our own. We almost never hear bishops or priests speak like this today!

Others will write adequately about the canonical, ecclesial, and political aspects of Archbishop Viganò's latest and very concise summary of the case.

As most of you know, I have fully affirmed elsewhere that I find his allegations credible and that they should be fully investigated. But in this post, I want to explore further the priestly qualities manifested in this third letter, qualities that are too often missing in action today.

To begin with, he has in mind the moral condition of souls. The archbishop warns in several places of the danger posed to the souls of the faithful by the silence and confusing actions of many bishops and priests and the pope. He laments that this, along with the homosexual subculture in the Church, "continues to cause enormous damage to the Church, to so many innocent souls, to young priestly vocations, and to the faithful in general."

A long time ago, in a galaxy far, far away, this was the first concern of most every priest: the moral condition of souls, including his own. Today, many bishops and priests, as well as many parents and other leaders in the Church, seem far more concerned with the feelings and emotional happiness of those under their care than with their actual moral condition. They worry more about political correctness and not upsetting those who engage in identity politics and base their whole identity on aberrant and sinful habits and disordered inclinations.

That a person be pleased and affirmed today is seemingly more important than that that person be summoned to repentance and healing or be made ready for Judgment Day. Passing and apparent happiness eclipses true and eternal happiness. Further, silence in the face of horrible sin and deferring to and fawning over powerful Churchmen and cultural leaders of this world seems to outweigh any concern for the harm caused to the souls and the lives of others.

Yes, too often, the only thing that really matters, the salvation of souls, is hardly considered. As others have rightly pointed out, this points to a loss of faith and a bland universalism wherein all, or the vast majority, attain to heaven. Further, the possibility of hell is all but dismissed—almost never preached, let alone considered a factor in how we should pastorally guide people.

In all of this, Archbishop Viganò still has that "old-time religion." He takes seriously Jesus' admonitions regarding Judgment Day, His many warnings about hell, and the absolute need to decide whom we will serve: God or the world, the gospel or popular culture, the spirit of the flesh. Viganò's final two paragraphs could not be clearer:

> *You can choose to retreat from the battle, to continue in the conspiracy of silence, and to turn your face away from the advance of corruption. You can invent excuses, compromises, and justifications that put off the day of reckoning. You can console yourself with falsehood and the illusion that it will be easier to speak the truth tomorrow, and then again the next day.*
>
> *Or you can choose to speak.*
>
> *You can have faith in the One who has said, "The truth will set you free." I do not say that it will be easy to decide between silence and speaking. I exhort you to consider which choice — on your deathbed and then before the Just Judge — you will not regret having made.*

This is powerful. I could be reading Saint John Chrysostom, Pope Saint Gregory the Great, or Saint Alphonsus Liguori. Honestly, I cannot recall many times having heard a modern bishop or even priest speak like this. There are exceptions, of course, such as the great Archbishop Fulton J. Sheen, but clarity is rare. I hope, too, that some of the deacons, priests, and bishops who might read this are saying, "I, too, am an exception. I often preach like this."

But my general experience tells me, from many who write to me, that their priests and bishops never mention mortal sin, hell, or judgment. And if they do preach on sin, they use abstractions and generalities, euphemisms and other safe terms, such as "injustice" and "woundedness."

In this letter, Archbishop Viganò writes as if he never got the memo to obfuscate and speak in cloaked and guarded ways, to speak in such hazy terms that no one really has any idea what you are saying.

Instead, the archbishop comes right out and says:

This very grave crisis cannot be properly addressed and resolved until we call things by their true names. This is a crisis caused by the scourge of homosexuality: in those who practice it, in its politics, and in its resistance to being corrected.

It is not an exaggeration to say that homosexuality has become a plague in the clergy that can be eradicated only with spiritual weapons. It is an enormous hypocrisy to condemn abuse, to speak of tears for the victims, and yet refuse to denounce the principal cause of so much sexual abuse: homosexuality.

It is hypocrisy to refuse to admit that this plague is caused by a grave crisis in the spiritual life of the clergy and fail to take the steps necessary to remedy it. . . .

There is overwhelming evidence that the plague of homosexuality in the priesthood is endemic, is spread through contagion, and has deep roots that are difficult to eradicate.

It is established that homosexual predators exploit their clerical privilege to their advantage. But to claim that the crisis itself is one of clericalism is pure sophistry.

Here, too, there have been very few bishops or priest willing to speak so clearly and to depart from euphemisms. There are exceptions, but they are too few. And, for a bonus round, the good archbishop even reintroduces an older term that has fallen out of use:

Undoubtedly there are also philandering clergy, and these offenses also create grave damage to the

souls of those who commit them, to the Church,
and to the souls of those whom they corrupt.

A philanderer is a "womanizer," one who, in an often-casual way, exploits a woman, but has little or no intention of marrying her. He will exploit her for his needs but not consider her as a person deserving of his ultimate respect and loyalty in marriage. Sadly, this, too, exists in the priesthood, but on a far more limited basis. Whatever the number or percentage of philanderers—one is too many—the much larger number of homosexual offenses (80 percent) in clergy sexual delicts shouts for attention.

But few, very few bishops or Vatican officials are willing to talk openly and clearly about it. This must change if any solutions are to be credible and the trust of God's people is to be restored. Excluding any reference to active homosexuality in the priesthood is like excluding any talk about cigarette smoking as a cause of lung cancer. It results in a pointless and laughable discussion that no one can take seriously.

Will any other bishops follow the lead of Archbishop Viganò and a few others, such as Bishop Robert Morlino? It remains to be seen, but credibility remains in the balance.

Viganò vs. the Vatican

Finally, Archbishop Viganò, in a Pauline sort of way, has taken up the necessary mantle of opposing Peter's (i.e., Pope Francis's) behavior to his face and publicly. Although some wonder why this is not done privately, the answer must surely be, "How could he approach Pope Francis privately?" Pope Francis has steadfastly refused to engage his questioners. He has taken up a policy of "weaponized ambiguity," and when legitimate questions are asked, they are greeted with silence. Far from answering his flock, he often refers to them as monsters, accusers, scandalmongers, and worse when they press for clarity and seek for answers and accountability.

How rare it is that other bishops are willing to speak out so clearly of their concerns. Only four cardinals issued the *dubia*. Why is this? Where are the rest? Only in recent weeks has the pope even hinted that there may be an allowable investigation in the Vatican Archives.

One must still ask: When? How? And to what extent? It will take a courageous insistence on the part of the faithful and the bishops to see this through.

In the end, I am deeply grateful for Archbishop Viganò's dose of "old-time religion." It is refreshing to hear an archbishop actually call sin by name, to show concern for the moral condition of souls, not just the emotional state, to warn of judgment and summon us all to decide — not just hide, obfuscate, and fret about "getting along" while souls are being lost.

It is hopeful that an archbishop of high reputation is willing to call the pope and the Vatican to account. This sort of leadership is too little in evidence today among the hierarchy and priests.[40]

---

[40] Monsignor Charles Pope, "Reflections on Archbishop Viganò's Courageous Third Letter," *National Catholic Register*, October 22, 2018, http://www.ncregister.com/blog/msgr-pope/reflections-on-archbishop-viganos-courageous-third-letter.

A Provisional Conclusion

✠ ✠ ✠

✠ ✠ ✠

We are at the end of this quick overview, which certainly
does not claim to be exhaustive but rather is useful for
reviewing certain key points of what may turn out to be
one of the most dramatic moments in the history of the
Church in our day. We would, however, like to consider
two more documents.

✠ ✠ ✠

I had decided, after reading it, not to write a review of a
huge instant-book that came out in late 2018 concerning the testimony of Archbishop Viganò. I do not much
care for token apologetics—the sort where you put your
money in a machine, and out comes the product that you
want—and after seeing that the testimonies reported in
the book are anonymous, I considered whether it might
not be better for me to follow the path of anonymity.

Also because, in this distressing affair, I continue to
be amazed that the only one who has come forward, with

courage and determination, is Archbishop Viganò himself, naming names and specifying others who could easily tell us what they know, since their conduct—beginning with the pope—has been called into question. Instead, all these people either remain silent (Ouellet excluded, but with results that were quite the opposite of what he wanted), or else they cloak in a cloud of mysticism their refusal to respond and clarify matters.

So I, too, wanted to be silent.

Then I saw that I was called into question, for something that is at best a distortion, and at worst an intended distortion. At a certain point I read: "But the one who intervened directly on the material of the dossier, convincing Viganò to use this form instead of an interview, was another long-time Vaticanist, Marco Tosatti."

This simply is not true.

I did not "convince" anyone, least of all Viganò.

When he came to my house at the end of August, I was convinced that we were going to conduct an interview. He told me, however, that instead he had decided to write a testimony, and that he would like me to read it. All I did for him then was to urge him to cut some things here and there, to amend certain passages to make them more understandable for the public, to decipher all the acronyms, and so forth. In sum, I did the ordinary work of editing an article that was written — entirely — by someone else, who felt in his conscience that he ought to defend a pope [Benedict] and his two colleagues [the former nuncios] who were not able to defend themselves from the insinuations contained in a biased article.

I thought that I had made all this sufficiently clear in the now more than two months that have passed since its publication. Why? Because the hypothesis that I had contributed to the composition of the testimony, even if it was not true and, as such, was a lie from the very beginning, was one of the first instruments the "negationist" party used to cry out that the Viganò testimony was an anti-Francis plot, carefully prepared by different contributors, and that even a long-time Vaticanist had participated in its composition.

This false claim may still be found today in the instant-book apologetic, reaffirmed without hesitation. But this is not surprising. The people of the publishing house to which the Vatican entrusted the composition of the book — just like the habitual commentator at *Avvenire* — needed to validate the thesis of an international and worldwide "plot," of which Viganò was merely the point of the spear.

Otherwise, we would have to wrap our heads around a more banal reality: that the pontiff did not heed the warning given to him by a nuncio about a despicable character who was one of his friends, of his same political line, who had helped him win election (as did other questionable persons, such as Cardinals Danneels, Murphy-O'Connor, Mahony, and Errázuriz Ossa — are we forgetting anyone?) and who would serve him as his counselor for the United States.

That same pontiff could get out of this impasse by two simple actions. First, he could respond, finally, to the personal question of Archbishop Viganò, and second, to shed light on the McCarrick case, he could establish an apostolic investigation, which would reveal who was complicit with McCarrick, who were his friends, and who financed him.

But the pope has not wanted to do this, despite the request of the American bishops to do so.

Why not?

This is what should be done, instead of commissioning token apologists to throw mud into the fans, anonymously.

✠ ✠ ✠

Finally, I would like to offer a brief message that Archbishop Viganò sent to the American bishops gathered for their assembly, who had just received the veto of the Holy See, preventing them from holding a vote on two important measures against abuse: a code of conduct for bishops and the institution of a committee of laymen to conduct investigations.

Strangely, as the American bishops received this ukase from the Holy See, the bishops in France entrusted to a layman the work of forming a lay commission to investigate abuse.

France, yes, and the United States, no?

Rather peculiar, no?

Soon afterward, the pontiff nominated three persons to organize the world summit on clerical abuse that would take place in Rome in February 2019: a Jesuit expert; Charles Scicluna, Archbishop of Malta and adjunct secretary of the Congregation for the Doctrine of the Faith; and—guess who—Blase Cupich.

And not Cardinal O'Malley, president of the Vatican Commission on Abuse.

While the American bishops were meeting, Archbishop Viganò wrote them a brief message, which seems to us to be an appropriate way to put—for now—a seal on this story, as we await further developments. It was written on November 13, 2018:

> *Dear brother bishops in the United States,*
>
> *I am writing to you to remind you of the sacred mandate that was given to you on the day of your episcopal ordination: to lead the flock to Christ. Meditate on Proverbs 9:10: "The fear*

of the Lord is the beginning of wisdom!" Do not behave like frightened sheep, but like courageous shepherds. Do not be afraid to rise up and to do the right thing for the victims, for the faithful, and for your salvation. The Lord will repay each one of us according to our actions and omissions. I am fasting and praying for you.

> *Archbishop Carlo Maria Viganò,*
> *your former apostolic nuncio*

Postscript

✠ ✠ ✠

✠ ✠ ✠

In February 2019, an unforeseen development happened.

Just as it was being announced that ex-cardinal Theodore McCarrick was deprived of the priestly state at the end of a rapid administrative procedure, the book *Sodoma* [*In the Closet of the Vatican*] was published, written by Frédéric Martel, a French activist for homosexual rights. Sowing suspicions and insinuations without reserve, the book asserts that the Vatican is the biggest (percentage-wise) homosexual community in the world.

Martel says that he spent one week per month in the Vatican as the guest of various prelates. He says that he was able to lean on Monsignor Battista Ricca, the director of Casa Santa Marta, who was named by the pontiff to be head of the IOR [Institute for Religious Works, the Vatican Bank]. Ricca was a diplomat, and his career was brutally cut short because of his involvement in homosexual affairs.

Martel claims that he was also helped and encouraged by at least four other prelates close to the pontiff. (It is certainly unusual that any person, much less a person with his history, and his literary and existential credentials, would be allowed to live at the Vatican for one week each month over a long period.)

Regardless, Martel is decisively in favor of the reigning pontiff; he affirms that the traditionalists who have taken positions contrary to homosexuality are for the most part themselves homosexual (without giving any proof); he attacks Cardinal Burke; in short, he cannot be counted among the critics of Pope Francis.

But Martel in his book—I have read the English text—provides resounding support for Archbishop Viganò!

In fact, he confirms that Pope Francis actually was informed by Archbishop Carlo Maria Viganò about the predatory past of McCarrick toward seminarians and young priests but says that the pontiff did not consider this fact important.

As a result, the pope not only lifted the restrictions that Benedict XVI had placed upon McCarrick (restrictions that were attested to by Cardinal Marc Ouellet as well as by Viganò) but also used him as a counselor for nominations in the United States. (Among the most recent confirmations—as if any were needed—of this claim are the promotion of Kevin Farrell to camerlengo and the entrusting of Blase Cupich with the organization of the recent summit on the abuse of minors.) The pope also used McCarrick as his personal envoy both in the United States (with Obama) and in China, Armenia, Cuba, and Iran.

In my opinion, this is an extraordinarily interesting case of "friendly fire," for if there is one person whom Frédéric Martel speaks well of, if not always enthusiastically, in his long work, let's repeat it — it's Pope Francis. Martel says that he met many times with the director of *La Civiltà Cattolica*, Antonio Spadaro, S.J. In the book, there is an interview with Spadaro, and there is also an interview with Cardinal Lorenzo Baldisseri, the great organizer of synods on the family and on youth, who is one of the pontiff's confidants and enjoys his trust. Thus, we ought to believe Martel, particularly because, in the following comment, he places the central phrase in quotation marks. Here is the little passage:

> Cardinals and bishops of the Roman Curia and of the American episcopate, according to him, took part in this enormous cover-up. It is an endless list of prelates, some of the most important in the Vatican, who were thus outed, rightly or wrongly as the case may be. (When the pope dismissed the accusations, his entourage indicated to me that Francis "was initially informed by Viganò that Cardinal McCarrick

had had homosexual relations with adult seminarians, but that this was not enough in his eyes to
condemn him.")

If Martel writes the truth, Viganò's charges are confirmed.
The need for an explanation of some sort by the pontiff
and the Vatican appears more necessary than ever.

Also, the administrative procedure that condemned
McCarrick was just that, only administrative. It did not
include, as would have a judiciary investigation, an inquiry
into the protection, complicity, and cover-ups that Mc-
Carrick enjoyed for years, right up to 2018.

But this is a lid that neither the Vatican nor the pontiff
seem interested in lifting anytime soon. Surely the declaration contained in the Martel book constitutes no small
element in this sad affair.

CRISIS Publications

Sophia Institute Press awards the privileged title "CRISIS Publications" to a select few of our books that address contemporary issues at the intersection of politics, culture, and the Church with clarity, cogency, and force and that are also destined to become all-time classics.

CRISIS Publications are *direct*, explaining their principles briefly, simply, and clearly to Catholics in the pews, on whom the future of the Church depends. The time for ambiguity or confusion is long past.

CRISIS Publications are *contemporary*, born of our own time and circumstances and intended to become significant statements in current debates, statements that serious Catholics cannot ignore, regardless of their prior views.

CRISIS Publications are *classical*, addressing themes and enunciating principles that are valid for all ages and cultures. Readers will turn to them time and again for guidance in other days and different circumstances.

CRISIS Publications are *spirited*, entering contemporary debates with gusto to clarify issues and demonstrate how those issues can be resolved in a way that enlivens souls and the Church.

We welcome engagement with our readers on current and future CRISIS Publications. Please pray that this imprint may help to resolve the crises embroiling our Church and society today.

Sophia Institute Press® is a registered trademark of Sophia Institute. Sophia Institute is a tax-exempt institution as defined by the Internal Revenue Code, Section 501(c)(3). Tax I.D. 22-2548708.